NATIONAL POLICE LIBRARY

2010448

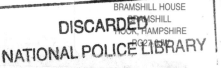
THE NATIONAL POLICE LIBRARY
BRAMSHILL HOUSE
BRAMSHILL
HOOK, HAMPSHIRE
RG27 0JW

DISCARDED

NATIONAL POLICE LIBRARY

D0314896

Best

Value

Uncovered

Best
Value
Uncovered

Essential skills for
The public sector

NATIONAL POLICE LIBRARY
NATIONAL
DISCARDED
FORCE
NATIONAL POLICY LIBRARY
LIBRARY

Jennifer Bean
Lascelles Hussey

Acc. no. 2010448

Clasmark DISCARDED

NATIONAL POLICE LIBRARY

HB PUBLICATIONS
(Incorporated as Givegood Limited)

Published by:

HB Publications
London, England

British Library Cataloguing in Publication Data

ISBN 1899448136

© HB Publications (incorporated as Givegood Limited) 2000. All rights reserved; no part of this publication may be reproduced, stored in a mechanical retrieval system, or transmitted in any form or by any means, electronic, photocopying, recording, or otherwise, without either the prior written permsision of HB Publications or a licence permitting restricted copying issued by the Copyright Licensing Agency, 90 Tottenham Court Road, London W1T 4LP. This book may not be lent, resold, hired out or otherwise disposed of by way of trade in any form of binding or cover other than that in which it is published, without the prior consent of HB Publications.

Printed and bound in England by Short Run Press Ltd.

Contents

INTRODUCTION 1

WHAT IS BEST VALUE? 3
Defining Best Value 3

HOW TO UNDERTAKE A FUNDAMENTAL
SERVICE REVIEW 11
The 4C's 14
Challenge 14
Compare 18
Consult 22
Compete 29
Conclusion 31

HOW TO ACHIEVE BEST VALUE SERVICES .. 37
Stages in Achieving a Best Value Service 37
Results Arising from a Best Value Review 38
Building Blocks for a Best Value Service 40

ESTABLISHING APPROPRIATE
PERFORMANCE INDICATORS 49
Performance Indicators 50
Developing Local Performance Indicators 51
Performance Measurement 57
Performance Monitoring 59

PREPARING A BEST VALUE PERFORMANCE
PLAN 63
Content of the Best Value Performance Plan 64
Format of the Best Value Performance Plan 66
Best Value Performance Planning Process 68
Linkages with other documents and available plans 70

SOLUTIONS TO EXERCISES 77

INDEX 85

Chapter 1

INTRODUCTION

Best Value Uncovered is a practical book that will enable the reader to work through the key stages involved in delivering the requirements of the Best Value regime. The organisations required by the Local Government Act 1999 to implement Best Value, should seek to achieve continuous improvement in the way in which they deliver services having regard to a combination of economy, efficiency and effectiveness. In order to do this, there will be a need for public sector organisations to work in partnership with other organisations, including those from the private and voluntary sector, and to develop a good relationship with the community whose needs they serve. Best Value is essentially about achieving best practice in the delivery of public services and, therefore, it is relevant for all organisations working in this sector.

There is already a great deal of information available on Best Value, along with assistance provided by central government departments and supporting agencies. This book intends to be a hands on tool that can be used by a manager in a practical way. It considers the Best Value process in a simple format and gives ideas and examples, missing from other literature.

Continuous improvement involves continuing organisational development and change. As such Best Value Uncovered can be instrumental in assisting individuals and teams realise this change by using the worksheets and exercises provided.

Most public sector organisations will find that the current environment of high expectations for service delivery and financial constraints make Best Value a challenging, but useful exercise, as it provides a process of regular reviews for all the services provided. These reviews, if correctly undertaken, will give rise to opportunities for innovation and creativity in the way in which services are provided such that value for money and customer satisfaction can be achieved.

This book is ideal for anyone working in or planning to work in a public sector environment, and who will have responsibility for delivering Best Value services. It is also relevant and useful for organisations that are not governed by the legislation on Best Value, as the principles of Best Value are transferable and can be used in all kinds of environments.

Chapter 2

WHAT IS BEST VALUE?

Defining Best Value

There are many concise definitions of Best Value, some of which are shown below:

Best Value is:

> *"better quality services at reasonable cost; and more say for local people"*
>
> > *(Your Services, Your Say, - Department for the Environment Transport and Regions (DETR))*

> *"A duty that will require local authorities to deliver the quality of service that local people expect at a price they are willing to pay"*
>
> > *(Minister for Local Government - Hilary Armstrong)*

> *"about improving the services we provide, being able to demonstrate high quality services and measuring the performance of what we do"*
>
> > *(London Borough of Lambeth)*

> *"to ensure that a real and positive difference is made to the services which local people receive from their Council"*
>
> > *(Leeds City Council)*

Best Value is a vision and as such it is open to various interpretations and definitions from different organisations. There is an overall theme that is reflected in all of the above, and that involves "services", "quality improvement" and "local people".

Even though there may be many different definitions of Best Value, there is a standardised approach that should be followed by all organisations trying to achieve Best Value. It centres around the performance management framework issued in the guidance provided by the DETR which can be summarised as follows:

Best Value Framework

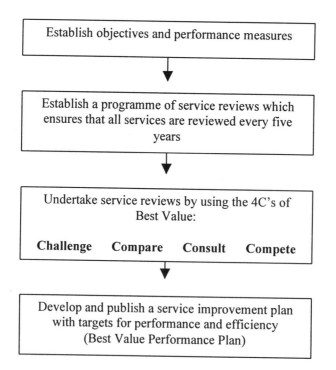

In order to ensure those organisations required to implement the Best Value framework do so successfully, central government have set up an independent audit and inspection process which will monitor how effectively organisations deliver on their performance plans. The Secretary of State has the power to intervene with those organisations which are failing to meet Best Value criteria. This intervention may give a wide variety of directions, including transferring responsibility to another authority or third party.

Identifying the key issues examined by the audit and inspection process, enables us to understand in a practical way, what is expected from Best Value.

Key Issues to be examined:

Organisational Aims:
- Are they clear and challenging?
- Are they being met by the current range of services being delivered?
- How are aims being turned into action?

Services:
- Has the need for them been fundamentally challenged and have local people been given the opportunity to scrutinise and challenge services?
- Has the current range of services been reviewed in the light of the wants, needs, and preferences of local people?
- Do the aims of the service reflect the views of local people and other stakeholders?
- Do the services take account of the diversity of the local community?

Service Provision:
- Has the use of current service providers been questioned in the light of other procurement options?

- How does the performance of the existing service providers compare with the top 25% of providers of the same or similar services?

- How does their performance compare with relevant and measurable government performance standards?

- What is their level of customer satisfaction and how does this compare with national satisfaction rates for the service?

- Are there systems in place to monitor service delivery and acquire feedback from customers and the local people?

- How competitive is the procurement process?

- Where the market place for services is currently weak or underdeveloped is there scope to develop it?

Consultation:
- Has extensive consultation been undertaken amongst the local people, service users, service providers, staff, and other key stakeholders?

- Have the results of consultations been taken into account and used as part of the service review and service improvement process?

Performance:
- Have measures of performance been established that will reflect the impact of change resulting from the 4Cs of Best Value?

- In addition to the national targets have performance targets been set at a local level?

Use of resources:

- Are plans to deliver, change and improve services communicated to all staff?

- Have adequate resources been allocated to achieve the plans?

- Are staff used to maximum efficiency and effectiveness?

- Are physical resources used to maximum efficiency?

- Do staff have personal targets and adequate training to ensure they can meet the overall performance levels that have been set?

- Are financial resources adequately managed and used to maximise service output?

- Are services being delivered cost effectively?

- Has cost effectiveness been demonstrated by subjecting services to external competition, or obtaining tangible evidence of value for money?

Service Improvement:

- Have targets been set to improve services and develop an implementation strategy?

- Are the targets set in the improvement plan challenging enough?

- In terms of performance against national standards and the critical success factors relating to delivered services, will the plan enable the organisation to get into the top 25% of defined organisations within five years?

The only way to successfully answer the above questions is to ensure that Best Value principles are embedded in all areas of the organisation. This means that Best Value will not only be represented in terms of the written output of a Best Value Performance Plan, but will also be dependent on the outcomes arising from change, service improvement and communication with local people.

As with any process, the starting point has to be "where are we now?" In order to establish this, the following diagnostic questionnaire can be undertaken to assess the current position, taking into account many of the issues raised in the previous paragraphs. This is a useful exercise whether or not you have previously been involved in the Best Value process, and acts as an initial audit for those embarking on implementing Best Value in their service area.

Exercise 1

Diagnostic Questionnaire
Where are we now - in terms of Best Value?

	Question	✓	x	n/a	Comments
1	Do you have a business plan with clear objectives?				
2	Have performance targets been set for continuous improvement?				
3	Have objectives been met consistently over the last 3 years?				
4	Have performance targets been met over the last 3 years?				
5	Have services been fundamentally reviewed within the last 3 years?				
6	Have service users been asked on a regular basis to give feedback on the services provided?				
7	Has data on customer satisfaction been collected, collated and used?				
8	Does someone monitor service delivery on a regular basis?				
9	Are quality standards being met at least 95% of the time?				
10	Have unit costs been calculated?				
11	Have unit costs been compared with those of other similar service providers?				
12	Have any benchmarking activities taken place?				
13	Given the market place, is the service currently competitive?				
14	Do staff have training plans that are regularly implemented?				
15	Is the latest technology for your service area currently being used?				
16	Have other providers ever been approached with respect to delivering all or part of the current service?				
17	Has the service ever been competitively tendered?				
18	Has the service undergone any significant changes in the last 3 years?				
19	Are there continuous service improvement activities?				
20	Do you consider that the service currently gives local people value for money?				

See page 81 for analysis of results.

Exercise 2

What is Best Value?

What does the vision of Best Value mean for your organisation/service area. Try to develop a concise definition of Best Value which could be easily communicated to staff and service users.

```
..............................................................................
..............................................................................
..............................................................................
..............................................................................
..............................................................................
..............................................................................
..............................................................................
..............................................................................
..............................................................................
..............................................................................
..............................................................................
..............................................................................
..............................................................................
..............................................................................
..............................................................................
..............................................................................
..............................................................................
```

Chapter 3

HOW TO UNDERTAKE A FUNDAMENTAL SERVICE REVIEW

The Best Value service review, should provide a basis for innovative approaches to service delivery and the development of performance targets which reflect continuous service improvement. Performance targets will have to take account of local and national standards. Authorities legally required to undertake service reviews, will have to review all their activities over a five-year period. The review process should be undertaken using the familiar 4C's framework (Challenge, Compare, Consult and Compete) which are discussed later in this chapter.

One of the first important steps is to identify who best to undertake the service review. This is a difficult question in some organisations and depends very much on a number of issue such as available resources and the existing organisational culture. Ideally the review should be undertaken by someone, or a group of people, who are distanced from the current arrangements for service delivery such that they can bring some objectivity to the process, however, this does not mean that a manager cannot adequately review his/her own service.

There have been a range of different models used for undertaking the service reviews, each of which have benefits and dis-benefits. The table below sets out some of the approaches.

Approach to service reviews	Benefits	Dis-benefits
Manager to review own service	• Knows the service well • Should already be aware of the inherent strengths and weaknesses • Should already have ideas for continuous improvement • Should know how to identify information requirements • Knows resources available to the service and the extent to which change can take place • Relatively low cost	• Closeness to the service may cloud objectivity • May wish to protect the status quo and secure existing jobs etc. • May have become devoid of new ideas and entrenched in habit • May not have the skills needed to undertake a review • Where a manager has existing duties, he/she may have insufficient time to adequately undertake the work required by the review
Manager to review another service within the organisation	• Good knowledge of the organisational environment • Has an arms length relationship with the service provider • Should be able to make an objective assessment • Relatively low cost	• May lack expertise • May lack knowledge of the service under review • May not have sufficient time to undertake the review • Managers own service may suffer as attention is deflected whilst undertaking the review
Panel of people undertaking the reviews comprising managers, users, Elected Members, etc.	• Mix of perspectives ensures that the review is well rounded and objective • Enables the workload of the review process to be shared • Involves a number of stakeholders in the process and hence outcomes will be more easily communicated	• May have conflicting views and priorities with respect to the service • May not have the skill or knowledge base • May be expensive to support and co-ordinate the process

Approach to service reviews	Benefits	Dis-benefits
Specialist unit established to undertake service reviews	• Consistent approach • Will be aware of the corporate priorities • Will gain an expertise and skill base in undertaking reviews • Will have a clear focus and objective to work towards	• May take a routine and inflexible approach and not understand the differences between services • Will not have an in-depth knowledge of the service under review • May be seen by services as not being truly objective in relation to the review, i.e. working to a corporate agenda rather than Best Value • May be an expensive option as staff and resources will have to be allocated to the unit
External consultants	• Will have expertise and knowledge of the process • Will ensure that the review meets the required standard as set out in the legislation • Will be objective and totally arms length • Will bring their experience of working with other organisations	• Not part of the organisation and may not understand the organisational culture • Will be expensive and subject to daily rates which may restrict the amount of work that the organisation can afford to commission • Can always walk away from the organisation and may not have any vested interest or long term commitment • Reviews have to be undertaken for all services on a rolling programme and the organisation will not benefit from the learning process

Whoever undertakes the service review, the choice should be made on a practical basis taking account of efficiency, effectiveness and economy (the 3 E's). In its 'Code of Audit Practice' the Audit Commission define these terms as:

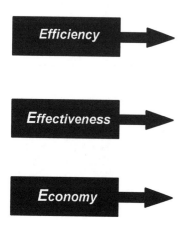

Producing the maximum output for any given set of resource inputs or using the minimum inputs for the required quantity and quality of service provided.

Having the organisation meet the citizen's requirements and having a programme or activity achieve its established goals or intended aims.

Acquiring human and material resources of the appropriate quality and quantity at the lowest cost.

The 4C's

Having established who undertakes the service review and how it will be conducted, the next stage will be to implement the 4C's in respect of the target service areas.

Each of the above stages are discussed in the following paragraphs.

Challenge

Definition: To ask, should the service be provided, if so, how should it be provided?

This stage can be understood by following this flow chart

CHALLENGE FLOWCHART

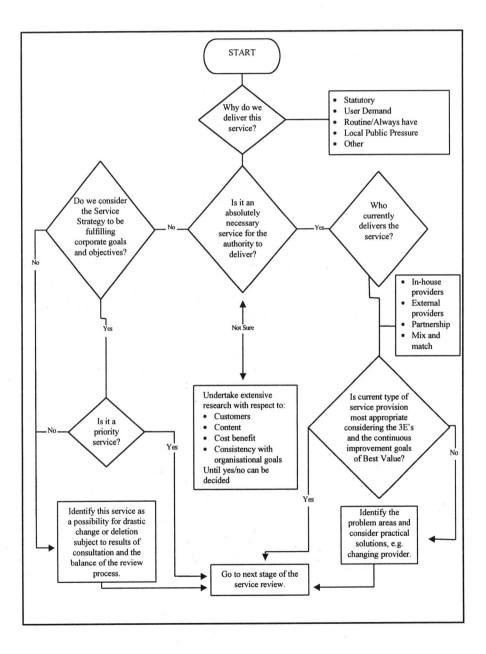

In order to adequately challenge why and how the service is being provided, there are a number of more detailed questions which should be answered. These include the following:

Why is the service being provided?	How is the service being provided?
• Is the service strategic to achieving corporate objectives? • Is the service in one of the organisation's priority areas? • Is the service targeted at one of the organisation's priority user groups, i.e. those in most need? • Is the service having a direct impact on improving the lives or environment of local people? • Are there any legal requirements which require service provision? • Is this service contingent upon any other service(s) being provided, and have those been challenged? • Do local people expect the service to be delivered (has this been asked?) • What are the possible implications of discontinuing the service?	• Is the service currently meeting the required performance and quality standards? • Is the service meeting performance targets? • What are the current strengths and weaknesses of the service? • What opinion do service users have of the current service provision? • Could the service be provided in another way, or be merged with another service? • Could the current level of service provision be altered? • Is there scope for the current provider to make any necessary service improvements? • Are there alternative service providers in the market place?

Having raised these questions, the next step is to:

- analyse the answers
- objectively make an assessment of the results
- decide whether the service should continue to be delivered
- decide how the service should be delivered or discontinued
- prepare an action plan to implement the above decisions

Information gained from the other remaining stages of the review may assist in answering these questions.

An example of the effective challenge of a service is set out as follows:

A local authority decided to undertake a service review of the "advice and information service" currently provided by a number of locally based one-stop shops which are multi-functional and have only recently become fully operational. In total, there are 6 shops strategically positioned around the area. The one stop shops provide a vast array of services, have an on-line computer system linking into all the departments, a massive database, and a cashiers service. One of the shops is located within a library, hence servicing an extremely wide range of users, many of whom are from priority groups within the authority.

The challenge process:

The authority formed a review group which comprised a user representative, a staff representative, a seconded manager from leisure services, and a local councillor who has a special interest in effective and efficient advice and information.

Having asked the types of questions listed above, the results showed that the shops are strategic and were formulated as a result of rationalising duplicated services provided by individual departments. The whole group were agreed that one-stop shops should continue but questioned how they should be delivered? Customer feedback suggested that opening hours and location were the key areas of concern. There were a number of options that came to light at this stage of the review:

~ Change opening hours to include Saturdays and late evenings (user suggestion)

~ Have a mobile shop, using one of the mobile libraries (staff suggestion)

~ Consider contracting out the service (manager suggestion)

~ Set more stringent performance targets (member suggestion)

Clearly having a team undertake the review, meant an abundance of ideas, however, the viability of the suggestions were uncertain at this stage. The group was still very open minded and found the challenge stage certainly made them think strategically and will be further informed by the other stages of the review.

Compare

Definition: **The performance of the service should be compared with others across a range of relevant indicators**

The compare stage of the review should be built into all modern public services. It is now common for performance indicators to be collected and published for most service areas, and hence there exists a good deal of information against which a service can be measured. This is not the case for all services and where there is a dearth of comparative data, the review process will have to incorporate additional work to identify such information.

Services should make comparisons with others on a range of areas including:

• Cost per unit of service

• Satisfaction ratings

- Productivity levels
- Successful outcomes (including prevention)
- Complaint levels
- Waste levels
- Quality systems, e.g. Investors in People, ISO9000, Charter marks, etc.
- Total expenditure
- Expenditure per head of population
- Percentage of total budget spent on the service
- Resource utilisation (staff, accommodation, equipment)

An organisation should set themselves the target of achieving the same standard of the best performer. Information for comparisons can be gained from the following sources:

- Performance indicators from the Audit Commission, CIPFA (Chartered Institute of Public Finance and Accounting)
- Benchmarking projects
- Joint working initiatives
- Exchanging information with other organisations
- League tables
- Other statutory data
- Independent research

It is clear that the task of making comparison for certain services may seem quite onerous, and it is quite possible that a substantial amount of time and money could be spent on seeking out the comparative data, particularly if the service represents a small percentage of the organisation's overall budget. A practical approach to seeking comparisons must therefore be taken.

Any comparative work undertaken should allow those performing the review to answer the following questions.

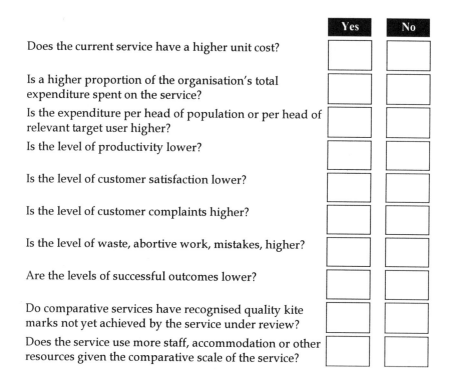

	Yes	No
Does the current service have a higher unit cost?		
Is a higher proportion of the organisation's total expenditure spent on the service?		
Is the expenditure per head of population or per head of relevant target user higher?		
Is the level of productivity lower?		
Is the level of customer satisfaction lower?		
Is the level of customer complaints higher?		
Is the level of waste, abortive work, mistakes, higher?		
Are the levels of successful outcomes lower?		
Do comparative services have recognised quality kite marks not yet achieved by the service under review?		
Does the service use more staff, accommodation or other resources given the comparative scale of the service?		

If the answer to any of the above questions is yes, then the reviewers need to consider whether there are valid reasons causing the difference. If not, they should then consider if it is possible to improve the service such that the gap can be bridged. It may be that the comparison shows a large differential which may indicate substantial changes are necessary to the existing service.

An example of the effective comparison of a service is set out as follows:

The manager of a training and development unit was tasked with undertaking a service review for her own service. She has completed the challenge phase of the review which has led her to believe that there are alternative ways of providing the current service. Some alternatives may include tendering out certain activities to third parties, along with the devolvement of some activities to service unit managers. There is a clear need for training and development support for the organisation, but the level of that support can vary tremendously and this was the focus of the 'compare' stage of the review.

In addition to comparing budget spends, unit costs, and productivity, she also compared the different approaches to delivering the service. This included a review of the successes/failures of the different models adopted by other authorities and similar organisations, including private sector companies of a similar scale and size to her organisation.

In order to ensure the validity of the comparative work, she looked at ten organisations and grouped them according to style of delivery. From this she produced a matrix which analysed the results over 4 key criteria for assessing the performance of the training and development service. The results of the comparison are set out below:

	Average unit cost per staff member trained/ developed (taking account of all expenditure)	No. of staff successfully trained/ developed as a percentage of all staff	Service achieved Investors in People	Productive days delivered by training and development staff per person per annum	Strategic influence on policy
The current service	£500	10	No	140	No
Other similar units delivering the same range of services in other organisations	£400	12	Yes	160	Yes
Contracted out services with in-house commissioning and quality control	£340	8	External Providers Yes	200	Yes

	Average unit cost per staff member trained/ developed (taking account of all expenditure)	No. of staff successfully trained/ developed as a percentage of all staff	Service achieved Investors in People	Productive days delivered by training and development staff per person per annum	Strategic influence on policy
Devolved services to departments with strategic advice to the corporate centre	£450	15	No	150	Yes
Part in-house delivery and part devolvement to departments	£400	16	Yes	150	No

Clearly there is scope for service improvement in all the areas compared, and it would appear that perhaps other ways of delivering the service may be more appropriate. The comparison element of the review is consistent with the findings arising from the challenge part of the review already undertaken by the manager. The manager is on a time-limited contract and therefore is in a position to be totally objective.

Consult

Definition: **To consult with local people, service users, staff, existing and potential external providers and partners, stakeholders and other relevant parties**

Consultation should be an on-going process and could take a variety of formats depending on the service being provided and the required information. Getting people involved with the types of services provided and the way in which they are delivered, is fundamental to Best Value. Consultation should cover all aspects of the review. Consultation needs to be wide ranging and include a wide cross-section of the community. Listed below is an example of the different types of interest groups that may be consulted, along with an explanation as to the purpose of the consultation:

People to consult	Purpose of consultation
Service users and potential service users	• Assessment of current service provision • Satisfaction levels • Perception of value for money • Ideas for service improvement and/or change • Participation in new service development • Identification of current and future needs • Encouraging community involvement
Existing service providers and partners	• Assessment of current service provision • Satisfaction levels • Ideas for service improvement and/or change • Participation in new service development • Identification of current and future needs • Quality standards and benchmarks • Reasons for current performance levels
Front line staff	• Assessment of current service provision • Satisfaction levels • Complaint levels - formal and informal • Ideas for service improvement and/or change • Participation in new service development • Identification of current and future needs • Quality standards and benchmarks • Reasons for current performance levels • Gaining support for change and the delivery of Best Value services
Members	• Vision, strategy, priorities, and leadership • Assessment of current service provision • Satisfaction levels • Complaint levels - formal and informal • Perception of value for money • Ideas for service improvement and/or change • Participation in new service development • Identification of current and future needs
Contingent and related service providers	• Assessment of current service provision • Efficiency of the interface between services • Satisfaction levels • Ideas for service improvement/or change • Quality standards and performance

People to consult	Purpose of consultation
Other service providers in the market place	• Perception of current service provision • Ideas for service improvement/or change • Possibility of collaboration/partnership
Local people	• Perception of current service provision • Perception of value for money • Potential for community involvement and support
Local businesses	• Perception of current service provision • Perception of value for money • Potential for business involvement and support

Depending on the group being consulted and the purpose of the consultation, several different modes of communication should be considered. These are discussed as follows taking into account the positive and negative aspects of each:

Consultation Method	Type of information gained	Positive Aspects	Negative Aspects
Postal questionnaires	Quantitative and qualitative data if a mixture of closed and open questions are included.	• Quantitative responses very good for analysis and statistics. • Qualitative data may be difficult to analyse, but does provide a written record of comments • Verifiable results not subject to interpretation • Information gained can be very specific, and targeted at particular aspects of the service • Relatively low cost	• Often a very low response rate if incentives to complete are not given, and/or questionnaire is too long • Questions need to be well drafted to avoid ambiguity • Questions may be biased to favour particular outcomes • Target group may become frustrated if bombarded with too many questionnaires

Consultation Method	Type of information gained	Positive Aspects	Negative Aspects
Telephone/ face to face questionnaires	As above	• Quantitative responses very good for analysis and statistics. • Qualitative data can be more detailed than above as follow up and probing questions can be asked to explain certain points • Verifiable results • Information gained can be specific and targeted • Higher response rates than postal questionnaires • Saves reading and writing on the part of the target group and hence is more accessible to the elderly, visually impaired etc.	• Cost of engaging researchers to undertake the telephone calls • Researcher may lead or pressure individuals to respond in a particular way • Certain questions may be emphasised more than others leading to bias
Face to face interviews	Main focus tends to be on qualitative data	• Can extract a lot more information about the service from an interview rather than from a questionnaire • Can ask probing questions to obtain opinions and explanations of comments made • Saves reading and writing on the part of the target group and hence is more accessible to the elderly, visually impaired, etc. • Group consulted can be very specific and targeted to obtain particular views on aspects of the service	• Requires skilled and trained staff • Expensive and time consuming • Difficult to analyse results, or make generalisations • May not cover the same numbers of people as the questionnaire approach (due to cost) • Interviews may be biased depending on the interviewer

Consultation Method	Type of information gained	Positive Aspects	Negative Aspects
Focus groups, local meetings, panels, etc.	Mainly qualitative data, but allows for the input of "experts"	• Group consulted can be very specific and targeted to obtain particular views on aspects of the service • Can gain collective opinions and consensus around particular issues • Allows for debate amongst the group and hence ideas and issues can be discussed and explored from a wide range of perspectives • Allows for special arrangements to gain input from hard to reach groups	• Need to be organised and co-ordinated which may be costly • Numbers may be restricted depending on time available • Large numbers at meetings may not give constructive feedback or the information required • When groups are brought together, they may end up being led by the strongest characters in the group and individual opinions may not be given • If groups are self selected, people coming forward may have a particular agenda, and hence skew the results
Internet web sites	Many sites have discussion forums which lend themselves to consultation of an open nature for qualitative data. On-line questionnaires can also be posted for quantitative data	• Makes use of the latest technology • Allows participation at any time of the day or night to suit the target group • Feedback is verifiable and not subject to interpretation • Same benefits as for questionnaires	• Initial set up may be expensive • Many constituents of the target group may not have access to the Internet (although some authorities have free access points in libraries etc.) • Some of the target group may find it difficult to use • Same difficulties as for questionnaires

Consultation Method	Type of information gained	Positive Aspects	Negative Aspects
Newsletters	Inserts, feedback sheets, questionnaires, competitions, and so on, can all be used as a means to consult the public and collect mainly quantitative data	• Low cost • Already have a set circulation on a regular basis • Opportunity to set consultation in context using an article to support the consultation mechanism • Same benefits as for questionnaires	• Low response from the readership without incentives • Same difficulties as for questionnaires

It is clear from the above, that there exists a large choice of options for consultation, and service reviews should choose the most appropriate method on the basis of practicality and effectiveness. The consultation method chosen, must ensure that certain groups are not excluded from the process, e.g. those for whom English is a second language (may need to consider different language questionnaires for some service areas), those with disabilities, young people, etc. Given that all services will need to undertake the consultation process, there may be benefits from collaboration. This will involve sharing information and results across services and, where relevant, with other organisations. Ideally a strategic organisational approach should be taken to the consultation stage; this is to avoid duplication and wasted resources.

An example of effective consultation is set out as follows:

The housing benefit service is having a Best Value review undertaken by an independent panel including the following:

- a Council Member with a special interest in housing benefit services;
- a senior manager from Council Tax services;
- a member of a local TMO (tenant management organisation);
- a seconded manager from the housing benefit service;
- a member of the Best Value unit (a small specialist support service unit).

To date, the five member panel have agreed on all the outcomes arising from challenging and comparing the service with other services provided by similar authorities. This authority has a relatively high level of low income groups and homelessness, and hence, housing benefit services are usually at full stretch with many of the target indicators not being met. This has led the team to consider alternative modes of service delivery including working in partnership with other local authority in-house providers, or externalisation. Part of the consultation strategy was to include feedback and information from other service providers in the public and private sectors. The other groups to be targeted and the approaches used included the following:

Group	Consultation Method	Cost
Current service users	Standard questionnaires and 3 targeted focus groups	Cost for questionnaire design and focus groups £3,000. Postage will be nil, as sent out with other correspondence
Potential service users	Individual telephone interviews with a small number of people identified through collaboration with other departments and agencies	Research and interview time £2,000
Staff	100% anonymous questionnaire circulation and 2 group meetings	Questionnaire development and a facilitator for the group meetings £1,500

The total cost of the consultation process was £6,500 (the budget set aside was £6,000). The analysis work was undertaken by the team (questionnaire analysis is part of the role of the Best Value unit). The results showed that the perception of the service was poor in a great many areas including responsiveness, accuracy, customer care, complaints, and communication. 90% of those consulted assessed the service as generally poor value for money. On the other hand, the consultation did bring forth many ideas for service improvements which could be implemented relatively quickly, and may make a difference to both service quality, efficiency and cost. These ideas came mainly from the staff and other service providers. The panel was divided as to the impact the results of the consultation had on their previous assessment of the service. They, therefore, agreed to wait until the compete stage of the review was completed before developing firm proposals for turning housing benefit into a Best Value service.

Compete

Definition: **To consider competition as a means of procuring Best Value services**

The competition element of the review process, is to ensure organisations keep an open mind as to who delivers the service. Having challenged the service, compared it to the best performance of comparable services, and consulted with all key stakeholders, users and local people, the question is "how can Best Value be achieved in a practical way?" It may be that although changes can be made to in-house services to improve service standards, the cost of change is greater than alternative modes of service delivery.

The competition element of the review is not about seeking ways to contract-out services, but rather to establish how a service should be delivered in order to give the best possible quality to the end user, and achieve continuous improvement through effectiveness, efficiency and economy, within the available financial resources.

The steps required to effectively undertake the compete element include:

- Identifying the market place for the service currently being provided, and the range of other service providers in that market place be they from the public, private or voluntary sector.

- Obtaining information on unit costs, benchmarks, performance indicators and so on, to assess whether the service currently being provided is competitive - remember that ideally like for like comparisons should be made and this is not always possible

- Obtaining information with respect to the differences between the current service and that being delivered by other parties performing at a higher standard or better value

- Examining the potential for joint ventures, partnerships, collaborations, etc. and whether or not this would have a positive impact on service quality, and cost

- Examining the potential for competitive tendering or contracting out all or part of the service and the impact this would have on service quality and cost

- Examining the potential of buying in aspects of the service as and when required and the impact this would have on efficient service delivery and cost

- Considering whether disposing of the service to an external provider would yield significant benefits and achieve Best Value (e.g. housing stock transfers)

Some of the work undertaken in the compare element of the review will be useful at this stage as it should have covered some of the same areas identified above.

There will be some services offered by authorities that do not have a "proper" market place because they are statutory in nature or command a monopoly position; i.e. only authorities undertake this type of activity. This does not mean that the compete element of the review is not undertaken with the same rigour as with other services. The only difference is the strategy developed to achieve a Best Value service, may not include direct competitive tendering or contracting out. Other strategies, such as partnerships, joint ventures, collaborations and mixed economy procurement, may be more appropriate. For example:

A planning service has been subject to a Best Value review and the compete element identified that unit costs were higher than at least 3 comparable authorities. Other aspects of performance were also below the standards required for Best Value. As a result of the compete aspect of the service review, the strategies that will be incorporated into the service improvement plan included:

❖ Use of consultants and temporary staff for peaks in work load

❖ Flexible working arrangements for staff

❖ Working in partnership with other neighbouring authorities

❖ Implementing performance management systems

❖ Collaborating with other agencies or the private sector to develop technology

❖ Identifying potential for increased income generation

❖ Investigating the potential for contracting out the administration aspect of the service

Conclusion

In order to undertake a successful service review the process should aim to achieve the following:

- objectivity in the review process

- comprehensive involvement from all parties with an interest in the service

- specific input from the current service providers and service users

- seek effective and appropriate advice

- question every aspect of the service

- take a medium to long term view

- consider all equality issues

- look inside and outside of the organisation

- ensure information is accurate and complete

- ensure any service improvement plan is practical, realistic, and can be implemented within a reasonable timescale

One of the keys to an effective Best Value review is the objectivity with which it has been undertaken. The outcome of the review should result in a way forward to delivering a Best Value service. This is discussed in detail in chapter 4.

Exercise 3

Best Value Review Process

In order to help decide the type of process your organisation/ department/ unit should adopt in undertaking an objective service review, answer the following questions:

Who should undertake the service review?

Identify who (individual or group) should undertake the review of your service	*State the reason(s) for your choice*

How should the service be challenged?
Think of 10 challenging questions which should be asked of your service (e.g. are we accessible to all our customers?, why do we complete our records in this way? are professionals undertaking administration tasks? do we cost more than our competitors?)

1 ⇨
2 ⇨
3 ⇨
4 ⇨
5 ⇨
6 ⇨
7 ⇨
8 ⇨
9 ⇨
10 ⇨

Who should the service be compared with?

Considering the market place in which your service operates (be that internal or external), draw up a list of at least 8 organisations that can be justifiably used for comparisons, even if the service being delivered is not exactly the same. These may include organisations in the public, private and voluntary sectors.

❶ ....

❷ ....

❸ ....

❹ ....

❺ ....

❻ ....

❼ ....

❽ ....

Who should be consulted?

List the key groups that should be consulted, and consider what information needs to be gained from the consultation process. Identify what practical consultation method can be used to gain that information.

Target Group	Information to be gained	Consultation method

What type of competitive options are relevant for this service?

State whether or not the following competitive options should be considered, giving your reasons.

Competitive option	Is it relevant? Yes/No	State reason
Competitive tendering		
Contracting-out		
Out-sourcing		
Disposal/Competitive sale		
Spot purchasing		
Preferred suppliers		
Partnerships		
Joint ventures		
Collaborations		
In-house restructuring against benchmarks		
Self-financing business units		
Mixed economy service provision		

Chapter 4

HOW TO ACHIEVE BEST VALUE SERVICES

Best Value should produce significant and continuous improvement, and as suggested in the previous chapters, is a vision, an approach, and a system of ensuring that an organisation is able to deliver the best possible services given the available resources. In order to achieve Best Value, an organisation may, therefore, require a totally different approach to service delivery. This may include working in partnership with others or procurement from third parties.

Stages in Achieving a Best Value Service

The stages in achieving a Best Value service can be shown in the diagram on the following page:

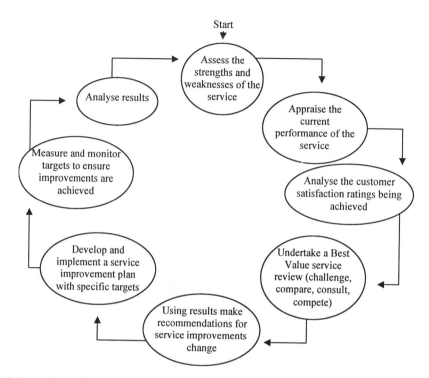

Note the diagram shows continuous flow back to the start stage, indicating that Best Value is an ongoing process which needs to be embedded within the organisation, such that it becomes a natural part of its culture reflected in its methodologies and outputs. It is required that all services will go through this process on at least a 5 yearly cycle.

Results Arising from a Best Value Review

The Best Value service will really come about from the results of the Best Value service review. Typically the results from the review may fall into one of the following categories:

- Best Value is currently being achieved with demonstrable continuous improvement year on year, optimum levels of efficiency, effectiveness and economy and high levels of customer satisfaction

- Several areas of service improvement are identified along with a practical plan of how those improvements can be achieved over time

- The service would benefit from a partnership or collaborative approach with identified third parties in all or some aspects

- There are alternative ways in which to procure the service that would better serve the Best Value objectives, i.e. spot purchasing, suppliers lists, short term contracts, etc.

- The service would benefit from part or all areas being openly subjected to contracting out or competitive tendering

- The current service requires a complete re-appraisal with respect to all areas from user profiles, service levels and service quality to performance indicators and unit costs

- The service in its present form cannot be justified for continued support and should either be disposed of or closed down

The categories lend themselves to a range of Best Value service delivery options described in the following paragraphs.

Best value service delivery options

The in-house provider
Services continue to be delivered by the existing provider working to a detailed service improvement plan with specific targets to be achieved and monitored

The external provider
Services are delivered to a service specification which sets the standards necessary to meet Best Value criteria with continuous improvement targets, and penalties for non achievement

The partnership, joint venture or collaborative approach
Clear agreement of responsibilities being shared between the parties and how they inter-relate with each other to achieve Best Value. Common goals and standards are set, monitored and measured to achieve continuous improvement, and a joined-up approach to service delivery which is seamless to the end user

The open market
Best Value service standards set in advance and used to benchmark any prospective supplier. The procurement process should seek to achieve best possible prices given the quality and quantities required to meet service improvement targets

A mixed economy
The same or similar service standards and continuous improvement targets set for both internal and externally provided services. The balance and mix of the two should maximise quality and output from the available resources and where possible create synergy and even further improvements

Each of the above options will be subject to cost and the available resources at the time.

Building Blocks for a Best Value Service

Best Value principles need to be realised at all times regardless of the service delivery option selected. To achieve this, a number of building blocks need to be in place. These include:

A Best Value culture:	Must be displayed from the top down. Openness, continuous improvement, performance management, innovation, good customer relations, effective communication, motivated staff.
Realistic targets:	Action plans that can be achieved.
Performance management:	Data collection on all aspects of activity including input, process, output and outcomes.

Unit costing and cost control:	Monitoring unit cost takes into account resource input (finance), and service output (productivity). Both need to be monitored to assess whether value for money is being achieved. A service area can be operating within budget, but if the output targets are not being achieved then it is not producing Best Value. Budget monitoring will only concentrate on the fact that the finances are under control. If the unit costs are being monitored, the lack of productivity will show up in the fact that the cost per unit will be rising or be above target, hence highlighting the value for money aspects.
Communication mechanisms for customers:	Ensuring that effective consultation processes are embedded in the service, and active customer and community involvement is sought wherever possible. Ideally this should be an organisational goal and not just for individual services.
Communication mechanisms for staff:	Ensuring that effective consultation processes are embedded in the service, and active staff involvement is sought wherever possible. Ideally this should be an organisational goal and not just for individual services.
Staff understanding of Best Value:	This should be transferred through training and the performance management framework within the organisation. Staff may need to change their attitudes as well as acquire skills and knowledge. It is important for staff to be able to translate the vision of Best Value into their day to day working environment.

An example of how a Best Value service can be achieved is given below:

The Scenario

An authority is determined to ensure Best Value makes a real difference to the way in which services are delivered. The authority had decided to use the Best Value legislation as a tool to effect organisational change and to really achieve efficiency, effectiveness and economy in all areas. The first step was to gain commitment from the top. The Chief Executive and the Senior Management Board (SMB) were in complete agreement with the aim to adopt a Best Value culture throughout the organisation. They were supported by the majority of Councillors and most importantly the leader of the Council who was very influential.

Each member of the SMB had responsibility for a major service area, e.g. education, social services, housing, etc. and a strategic responsibility for a support service such as human resources, communications, marketing, finance and so on. This structure had already resulted in major gains by breaking down departmental barriers on strategic issues, and achieving savings by eliminating duplication and creating economies of scale.

The SMB decided to assess the strengths and weaknesses of all service areas and the organisational performance as a whole, including looking at current performance, customer satisfaction and the achievement of targets set out in service plans. This assessment would enable them to map out the Best Value Service Review Programme, and put in place a Best Value planning process which would be ongoing and embedded within a performance management structure. The SMB decided that they would do this work with the Managers Forum which was an established group representing all service areas across the authority. The results of the assessment would be communicated to all staff via service managers and a representative range of service users via the user group network (UGN), a body already established with representation from users of most services. Feedback would be gained from staff using the quarterly staff survey (a coded survey to ensure completeness where names need not be entered). Feedback from the UGN would be achieved by the representatives consulting the community in the most appropriate ways and completing a feedback form for analysis.

The Strengths and Weaknesses

The assessment resulted in identifying the following strengths that would form the building blocks for the Best Value culture:

❖ Strong leadership from management with clear focus and vision

❖ A commitment from the top to Best Value principles

❖ The existence of a corporate plan based on service plans

❖ Performance appraisals in place and being successfully operated

❖ Most parts of the organisation have, or nearly have, achieved Investors In People

❖ A successful quarterly staff survey which results in service improvement ideas

❖ The establishment of the UGN as a means to promote wider consultation

❖ A marketing and communications strategy to promote the authority and its work internally and externally

❖ An annual community survey to all households and a twice-yearly service survey

❖ Performance indicators at all levels for all functions and services

❖ All support service areas have been market tested along with many other direct services

The apparent weaknesses, which would help determine the objectives and priorities for the service reviews, were as follows:

❖ Inadequate staff training with respect to skills, knowledge and attitude, particularly in areas such as customer focus

❖ Insufficient funds in some service areas due to poor budget setting

❖ Performance targets not met in some service areas

❖ Some service areas appear to have high unit costs in comparison to other authorities and relevant organisations

❖ Although customer satisfaction with the authority as a whole is above average, some service areas have below average satisfaction ratings

❖ Income is not being maximised and income collection is poor

❖ Not all services have fully documented service standards for monitoring purposes

❖ More thought needs to be given to the relevance of some of the current locally determined performance indicators

❖ The performance culture has not been adopted by all members of staff and appears to be particularly weak in two departments

❖ Council Tax levels are still relatively high given the nature of the authority

The Recommendations

As a result of the assessment, the following recommendations were made and communicated to staff and users for consultation.

❖ A new organisation wide training programme (in addition to existing staff training and development commitments) for all staff with short workshops covering the themes of:

~ Best Value
~ Performance management
~ Customer focus
~ Quality standards

❖ A revision of the budget setting process to take account of service priorities, Best Value Service Reviews and demand led budgets

❖ A five year programme of fundamental service reviews for Best Value, loosely based on a "worst first" principle, taking account of current performance, customer satisfaction ratings, unit costs, strategic importance to the authority, and the authority's priorities. The first 10 being:

~ Environmental health
~ Refuse collection
~ Libraries
~ Children services
~ Mental health services
~ Facilities management services
~ Cleaning services (currently under contract)
~ Housing repairs and maintenance
~ Payroll services (currently a Direct Service Organisation)
~ Educational advisory services

The service review panels to be made up of two elected members, a staff representative, a user representative and a member of the Corporate Best Value Review Team (to ensure consistency, objectivity, and that legal requirements are met).

❖ A greater emphasis on income generation and collection with a named officer responsible to achieve new targets; this strategy will facilitate council tax reductions

❖ Locally determined performance indicators, to be reviewed by each service on an annual basis with respect to their relevance to service delivery and service delivery improvement

The Results

Arising from the staff survey, there was a broad consensus with all the recommendations except for the make up of the service review panels; staff suggested that more than one staff representative be present. This point was accepted.

The result arising from the consultation with users via the UGN highlighted a number of different service priorities. It appeared that libraries were not considered to be a high priority for review, but the homelessness unit seemed to be at the top of many peoples list. This was most probably because of some high profile incidents that had been widely publicised with respect to bed and breakfast provider payments for very poor quality services. The libraries were an authority priority because of the impact it may have on a key financial strategy for income generation. In order to take account of local opinion and concern, the homelessness unit was moved from the year two round of reviews to year one.

Having undertaken this initial process, the results of the Best Value Service Reviews were excellent. Innovative recommendations were made, with realistic action plans to meet realistic targets over time, and to achieve real service improvement. The Best Value review team are responsible for monitoring the action plans and reporting on the results.

The authority could see the impact of the staff training on the standard of services delivered across the organisation and customer satisfaction ratings were up in all areas.

It was agreed that the assessment process should be undertaken on an annual basis as a means of reviewing the current situation, appraising performance and identifying Best Value Service Reviews; any major changes should be consulted on with staff and users. The authority considers that this will ultimately lead to all services being delivered by the organisation meeting Best Value principles.

Exercise 4

Achieving Best Value

The service improvement plan is key to achieving a Best Value service over time.

Whether or not a Best Value service review has been undertaken on your service to date, state in your opinion the key areas in which you consider services could be improved. What targets would you set, over what timescale, and how could the targets be monitored to ensure success?

Area of service for Improvement	Target	Timescale	Monitoring Process
....	....	....	....
....	....	....	....
....	....	....	....
....	....	....	....
....	....	....	....
....	....	....	....
....	....	....	....
....	....	....	....

Area of service for Improvement	Target	Timescale	Monitoring Process
....	....	....	....
....	....	....	....
....	....	....	....
....	....	....	....
....	....	....	....

Review each of the above for their practicality and revise if necessary.

47

2

Chapter 5

ESTABLISHING APPROPRIATE PERFORMANCE INDICATORS

In order to understand performance indicators, in the context of Best Value, it is necessary to make reference to the Government's definitions of performance indicators and to establish how those relate to performance standards and targets. The definitions are given as follows:

Performance indicator
the measure of a Best Value authority's performance in exercising a function as specified from time to time by legislation

Performance standard
the minimum acceptable level of service provision which must be met by a Best Value authority in the exercise of a function and measured by reference to a <u>performance indicator</u> for that function. A failure to meet a performance standard will be judged as failing the Best Value test for that service function

Performance target
the level of performance in the exercise of a function that a Best Value authority is expected to achieve, over a minimum period of a year and measured by reference to the performance indicator in relation to that function

(Performance Indicators for 2000/2001 - DETR)

The issues of performance indicators, measurement and monitoring are discussed in further detail below.

Performance Indicators

Best Value authorities have to implement a family of performance indicators. These are:

- **Local performance indicators -** These indicators are in addition to those that have to be reported to government. They should reflect local service objectives and standards, and will enable the measurement of local needs and priorities

- **Best Value Indicators -** These are national performance indicators which should reflect the national interest in the delivery of local services. They will enable comparisons to be made between the performance of different authorities, and within the same authority over time

- **Audit Commission Indicators -** These are national indicators that have been collected for several years and may be amended to take account of Best Value and change.

- **Other indicators set by Government Departments -** These are requested as part of the data collection requirement of these departments

The Best Value indicators are being developed in a way that takes account of other existing national indicators and as such will provide an integrated framework for authorities, such that duplication is minimised.

Performance indicators should provide a rounded view of service performance which reflects service users actual experience. The government has established five dimensions of performance to be considered as a basis for the range of Best Value performance indicators. These are:

strategic objectives:	why the service exists and what it seeks to achieve
cost/efficiency:	the resources committed to a service; the efficiency with which they are turned into outputs
service delivery outcomes:	how well the service is being operated in order to achieve the strategic objectives
quality:	these indicators will explicitly reflect users' experience of services
fair access:	ease and equality of access to services

(Performance Indicators for 2000/20001 - DETR)

Developing Local Performance Indicators

As every authority has an element of uniqueness, local performance indicators should be developed in addition to those specified by the Audit Commission and the government. The way in which services are delivered, the mix of client groups, and the management structure will often require specific areas of performance to be measured. Local people will have differing needs and priorities for different services over time. These issues should be taken into account when developing local performance indicators.

Local performance indicators should also assist managers to manage the service in a way that can show demonstrable service improvement. This may mean some performance indicators are developed to look at specific issues which are only relevant to that service. However, a practical approach should always be taken and the number of performance indicators should not become so large that measurement and monitoring becomes such an onerous, costly and time consuming task in its own right.

An approach to identifying appropriate performance indicators is described below:

Step 1	→	Establish the service objectives
Step 2	→	Identify the elements of each stage of the service, i.e., input, process, output and outcome
Step 3	→	Given the quality standards to be achieved, consider and list the key factors that determine management, staff and customer satisfaction within each area of the service.
Step 4	→	Consider the practicality of collecting information with respect to the key factors, i.e. what is currently being collected, what changes can be made in order to collect the most appropriate information
Step 5	→	From the above process, prepare a list of performance indicators and taking account of the service objectives, management requirements, government and Audit Commission indicators, select the most appropriate local indicators
Step 6	→	Develop and continuously review the systems used to collect the data needed to measure the performance indicators
Step 7	→	Review list of local performance indicators on a regular basis to reflect changes to the service objectives, service delivery approach, client groups, legislation, and so on

Adopting the above approach, an example of developing local performance indicators is given as follows:

A local authority social services department, has recently established a multi-disciplinary youth offending team and has named it the YOT service. Because this is a new configuration of the old youth justice service, the manager wishes to develop a range of local performance indicators to start as she wishes to go on. She began by looking at one aspect of the service with a view to using this as a model for all the other areas.

SERVICE DESCRIPTION

The Pre-Sentence Report (PSR), in respect to a young offender, is developed for presentation to the court. The report contains recommendations considering all available options from supervision orders to custodial sentences.

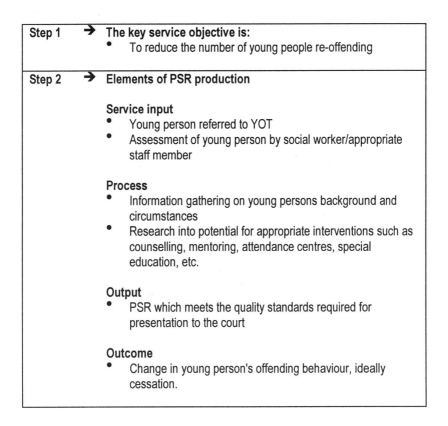

Step 1 →	**The key service objective is:** • To reduce the number of young people re-offending
Step 2 →	**Elements of PSR production** **Service input** • Young person referred to YOT • Assessment of young person by social worker/appropriate staff member **Process** • Information gathering on young persons background and circumstances • Research into potential for appropriate interventions such as counselling, mentoring, attendance centres, special education, etc. **Output** • PSR which meets the quality standards required for presentation to the court **Outcome** • Change in young person's offending behaviour, ideally cessation.

Step 3	➔	**Key factors for satisfaction**

Service input
* Number of young people seen
* Time taken
* Cost
* Assessment standards met
* Client treated fairly
* Equalities policies adhered to
* Client feedback
* Complaints

Process
* Time taken
* Cost
* Accuracy and completeness
* Quality standards met
* All options considered
* Client treated fairly
* Equalities policies adhered to
* Client feedback
* Complaints

Output
* Time taken
* Cost
* Accuracy and completeness
* Quality standards met
* Deadlines met
* Recommendations accepted by court

Outcome
* Number of PSR recommendations being accepted and implemented
* Number of clients re-offending
* Client satisfaction with the service
* Complaints
* Total costs
* Youth crime reduction

Step 4 ➜	The current position is that:

- Very little information is being collected on the time it takes to do things and hence it is very difficult to identify the costs,(which are mainly time spent), and responsiveness.
- There is a paper file record of how many young people have PSR's and file records are kept with respect to meetings held, letters written and so on.
- Quality standards have not been set in all areas of the work but are currently being developed
- Very little monitoring of equalities issues
- No current information on customer satisfaction
- Records of complaints are kept
- Number of re-offenders within a certain period could be identified, but only in a time consuming way as no database of client information has ever been created
- Youth offending statistics are available, but only in general terms

In order to implement meaningful performance indicators, there is a clear need to make changes to the nature of the information collected, and how it is recorded. Recommended changes will include:
- Introduction of time sheets to be recorded and analysed using an appropriate PC based system
- Development of client feedback sheets to be completed after each intervention stage
- An annual staff and customer survey focusing on satisfaction, equalities issues, and service improvement
- Completion of the in-house quality manual
- Development of a client database, which includes the outcomes of each case
- Unit costs to be calculated for each case, for example, hourly rates of professional staff time

All these changes are practical, however a timetable for change will need to be developed and implementation will have to be phased in.

Step 5	➜	Having considered the results of the previous steps, the following performance indicators appear most appropriate for measuring and monitoring the performance of this service area:

- Number of clients seen during the year
- Cost per client seen
- Time taken to prepare a PSR
- Unit cost of preparing a PSR
- Quality standards met (in all areas)
- Client feedback on process
- Number of re-offending clients within a 2 year period
- Percentage of PSR recommendations being accepted in court
- Level of customer satisfaction
- Level of complaints

Although other indicators could be developed, it was considered that focusing on these 10 would be a good starting point. This is especially the case given the number of new systems now required in order to obtain the relevant information for measurement.

Having identified the type of indicator that is most appropriate, a performance target has to be set which will ideally demonstrate measureable service improvement. Targets can be developed with reference to past performance, the performance of other authorities and organisations with the same or similar service, and, if available, standard best practice benchmarks. Some of the national Best Value performance indicators have set a framework for certain targets, such as being in the top quartile of authorities. This type of target requires authorities to know the levels being achieved by the top 25% of authorities such that they can strive to be within that band. All targets should, however, be locally determined. For example, the emergency services have the following indicators:

| Performance Indicator | Locally Determined Targets | | |
(Performance indicators for 2000/2001 - DETR)	Target this year	Level Achieved	Target next year
Number of public disorder incidents per 1000 population	20	18	15
Percentage of 999 calls answered within 10 minutes (local response time)	90%	87%	92%
Percentage of recorded crimes detected	85%	80%	85%
Number of substantiated complaints per 1000 detainees	10	15	10

Ideally, the level achieved should equal or exceed the target for each performance indicator, if not, this needs to be taken into account when developing the target for the following year. Year on year, targets set for each performance indicator should become more rigorous, hence ensuring continuous service improvement.

Steps 6 and 7 of the above process, should then be followed to review the effectiveness of the performance indicators.

Performance Measurement

This can be successfully achieved if:

- Adequate data collection systems are in place

- The data is timely, accurate and complete

- The data can be easily analysed and manipulated

The task of performance measurement, needs to be built into the organisations performance management system such that it is not regarded as a time consuming exercise, but part of the every day work routine. Technology can be of great assistance with respect to data collection and analysis, and ideally a computer programme can be developed such that the level of performance can be automatically calculated.

Performance measurement techniques can be illustrated by using the previous example, where the YOT service identified 10 performance indicators.

Performance Indicator	Performance Measurement
Number of clients seen per year	Record of each client referral ideally held on a database system, and production of an end of year total
Cost per client seen	Take cost of the service and divide by the number of clients
Time taken to prepare a PSR	Use time sheet analysis where PSRs are a separate activity code and analyse number of staff hours charged to this area of work
Unit cost of preparing a PSR	Calculate the total cost of PSR work by calculating the total cost of each hour of staff time spent producing PSRs, and divide this by the number of PSRs produced during the year
Quality standards met (in all areas)	Record on the client database whether or not the quality standard was met for each aspect of the PSR development and presentation. Several measures can then be calculated, for example, what percentage of PSRs produced fully met all quality standards.
Client feedback on process	Information collected from feedback sheets should ideally be entered onto a database for easy analysis. Measurements will depend on the questions asked on the feedback sheet, for example, if an equalities question was raised, the percentage of clients seen who felt they were fairly treated could be calculated; an ethnicity breakdown could also be incorporated.

Performance Indicator	Performance Measurement
Number of clients re-offending within a 2 year period	This information can be extracted from the client database and presented as a percentage of the total number of clients seen
Percentage of PSR recommendations being accepted in court	The outcome of the PSR could be recorded on the database, and then a comparison made of the total number of PSRs written against those accepted
Level of customer satisfaction	Customer satisfaction ratings can be gained from analysing the information on the feedback sheets and the annual survey
Level of complaints	This can be measured by referring to the complaints register

The results of the performance measurement should be compared to the set targets. An assessment can then be made as to if targets have been met, taking into account any factors that may have had an impact on the results.

Performance Monitoring

Performance monitoring is an ongoing process which should be incorporated into the way in which services are managed. Certain key performance indicators should be measured on a monthly basis such that the manger can consistently monitor exactly what is happening over a period of time. This level of monitoring will enable the manager to quickly identify if and why targets are not being met, and hence allow the appropriate action to be taken.

The performance monitoring cycle should include the following:

Comparing actual performance with target performance	Identifying the cause of any differences	Taking appropriate action	Measuring the impact of the action on actual performance

If a fundamental problem exists resulting in performance targets not being met, the manager should seek to advise more senior management and fundamental change may have to take place. This process is critical to the success of Best Value which expects continuous service improvement and requires services to be delivered in the most efficient, effective, and economic way possible.

Exercise 5

Identifying Performance Indicators

Using the steps set out in this chapter, develop or re-confirm the most appropriate performance indicators for any aspect of your service.

Step 1	➔	Establish the service objectives
Step 2	➔	Identify the elements relating to the service, input, process, output and outcome
Step 3	➔	Given the quality standards that have to be achieved, consider and list the key factors that determine management, staff and customer satisfaction at each stage of the service

Exercise continued on the next page

Step 4	→	Consider the practicality of collecting information with respect to the key factors, i.e. what is currently being collected and what changes can be made in order to collect the most appropriate information
Step 5	→	From the above process, prepare a list of performance indicators and taking account of the service objectives, management requirements, government and Audit Commission indicators, select the most appropriate local indicators

Chapter 6

PREPARING A BEST VALUE PERFORMANCE PLAN

"Performance plans will provide local people with a clear practical expression of an authority's performance in delivering local services and its proposals to improve."
(This is a quote from the DETR)

All authorities affected by the Best Value legislation, are required to produce an annual Best Value Performance Plan. Although the plans should contain certain fundamental elements, there is no specific format for the content of the plan. Section 6 of the 1999 Local Government Act, sets out matters that should be included in the Performance Plan. These matters include a clear statement on:

- what services an authority will deliver to local people

- how it will deliver them

- to what level services are currently delivered

- what future levels of service the public should expect

- what action an authority will take to deliver those levels and over what timescale

Content of the Best Value Performance Plan

The draft guidance on the content of the Best Value performance plan, produced by the DETR, suggests the following key areas for inclusion:

A summary of the authority's objectives in respect to its functions
- *Overall vision*
- *Community strategy*
- *Service priorities*
- *Financial strategy*

A summary of current performance
- *Against targets*
- *Comparative Performance (e.g. against national average)*
- *Successes and Failures*
- *Progress made put into context*

A comparison with performance in previous financial years
- *Performance indicator results compared year on year*
- *Performance indicator results compared with the best performing authorities*
- *Explanation and analysis of trends*
- *Comparisons made put into context*

A summary of the authority's approach to efficiency improvement
- *Corporate approach*
- *Individual Service approach*
- *Potential and scope for improved efficiency and effectiveness*
- *Target level of efficiency gains*

The key results of completed reviews
- *Reports on reviews undertaken during the previous year*
- *Report on reviews in progress*
- *Results of consultation*
- *Explanation of outcomes and action plan to achieve recommended targets*

A plan of action for substantially changed targets or post review targets
- *Specify, in summary, how targets will be met within a time frame*
- *Identify key stages where progress can be measured and monitored*
- *Identify responsibility and accountability for achievement*

A response to audit and inspection reports
- *Include recommendations from the pervious year's audit report*
- *Highlight changes that have been made as a result*
- *Indicate future changes to be made as a result*

A consultation statement
- *Comment on the form and type of consultation carried out*
- *Identify the number and types of groups, individuals, etc. involved*
- *Analyse the results of the consultation*
- *Give information on improved and future planned consultation*
- *Provide an opportunity for feedback and local involvement*

A financial statement
- *Summary of financial accounts*
- *Summary note of turnover and profit/loss of significant trading operations (for which separate accounts are required)*
- *Summary of budgeted income and expenditure for the year ahead (based on information sent with council tax statements)*
- *Details of major capital projects and investments*

(Only main headings taken from DETR draft guidance on implementing Best Value)

Format of the Best Value Performance Plan

The exact format has not been specified and organisations should develop a format that best suits their particular target audience. Given the amount of detail required for the plan, some plans may become very lengthy and a summary may be most appropriate for general circulation, with the full plan being available for public view at strategic locations. With respect to public presentation, the format of the plan should be:

- Easy to read and understand

- Concise

- Clear

- Up to date

- Highly visual (use graphs, charts, pictures, and so on)

- Focused on performance, past, present and future

- Accessible to all parts of the community

To ensure the plan is accessible to all parts of the community, the authority should consider the ways in which the plan is to be communicated, including:

- Inclusion in local newspapers

- Inclusion in local/area newsletters

- Sent out with Council Tax

- Copies available in Council offices, community centres, libraries, leisure centres, schools etc.

- Held on the Internet

- Being made available in different formats, e.g. local languages, large print, braille, tape, etc.

The importance of feedback and successfully engaging with the community to secure their involvement cannot be overstated. Approaches to achieve this may include:

- Questionnaires

- Feedback sheets attached to the plan

- Interactive web sites

- Focus groups

- Community Forums, Panels, Estate Management Boards, School Governors etc.

- Staff survey

Including incentives to feedback usually increases participation, such as a prize draw, competitions, discounts, vouchers, and so on.

Best Value Performance Planning Process

Having considered the content and format of the plan, organisations also need to consider their approach to developing the plan. Whatever approach is taken, it should be consistent year on year such that real comparisons can be made. That is not to say, however, that the approach taken cannot be modified and improved over time. Organisations have already developed their own approaches, but, each must establish the best fit given the existing culture and available resources.

Irrespective of the approach taken, the planning process should include the following features:

Leadership

It is important that the process is led. This leadership may come from an individual or a team. In the case of an individual it may be a chief officer, a councillor, or even an outside expert. A team may include a mix of one or more of the following; top tier officers; a cross section of officers and staff; elected members; external experts; local representatives; and service users. With leadership comes responsibility and accountability for ensuring that the plan is produced within the timescale, and is a useable, workable document that meets all the requirements of Best Value.

Developing the vision

There must be a clear vision as to the type of organisation the authority wishes to be. It may be a vision that has not yet been reached but it should be achievable and realistic in the medium term. The vision must be informed by the views of the local community and reflect their wishes with respect to services, the environment, and the culture they wish to see presented by the authority. The planning process should, therefore, include broad and regular consultation and the results should be reflected in the vision statement.

Setting priorities

All organisations have to work within constraints, especially resource constraints, and hence priorities must be established with respect to the overall objectives that can be realistically achieved by each service area. These objectives will enable the authority to realise the vision over time and should be SMART (Specific, Measurable, Achievable, Realistic and Time-related) in nature, such that progress can be measured. Again the priorities need to be set in a way that reflects the needs of the local community.

Setting targets

There should be national and locally developed performance indicators against which targets should be set. The targets should reflect service development and improvement over time and should be ambitious but realistic. The process of setting targets is an internal one, but should involve management and staff within each service area in order to obtain a commitment to achieving those targets.

Performance measurement

Every planning process should include an assessment of the current position. Part of that assessment must include identifying current performance levels, using the performance indicators as a base, and comparing against the targets that had been set. This allows for an analysis of whether or not targets have been achieved and the underlying reasons that have led to the current position. This information can then feed into the priorities and target setting stages of the process. The results arising from assessing current performance may also affect the service review timetable; this will identify those services most in need of review.

Service reviews

Best Value requires regular reviews of all services over an agreed time period. The planning process should ensure that service reviews are being carried out within the correct time frame and the results incorporated into the plan. The results of service reviews should be reported and also used to have a real impact on the priorities and target setting elements of the planning process.

Action planning

This is the most tangible element of the planning process because in order to realise the vision, it requires a clearly thought out range of activities. These activities require implementation in order to achieve the objectives stated in the plan. The action plan may refer to other planning documents for detail, but should give the reader a clear indication of how the authority intends to move forward on all the issues highlighted in the plan. This part of the process should also identify how the action plans will be monitored and tangible success factors need to be specified, ideally linking into the performance targets.

The planning process will only be successful if:

- There is wide ranging involvement including elected members, managers, staff, users, and the local community

- There is wide ranging communication in a way that is understood by all of the above

- There is commitment to achieving the objectives and targets set out in the plan

- There is constant measurement, monitoring and review of the results being achieved

- There is flexibility and a willingness to change when required

- It is understood that the plan will really make a difference and is not just a paper exercise

Linkages with other documents and available plans

The Best Value Performance Plan should fit into the hierarchy of plans that may already exist within the organisation. Typically there may be:

A Community Plan

A Corporate Plan

A Financial Plan

Departmental Business Plans

Service Plans

Individual unit plans
(such as business units, schools, cost centres, etc.)

Other operational and strategic plans
(such as marketing, communications, human resources, asset management, etc.)

It is important that all the plans produced should be consistent with each other, and ideally prepared following a logical timetable which ensures that the information pertinent to each is available at the right time. There needs to be both a top-down approach which ensures leadership in the form of a corporate vision and strategy from which service areas can develop. Similarly, a bottom-up approach is necessary which ensures services are developed taking into account the needs of the local community. To achieve this an authority will require:

- A shared vision

- Clear measurable objectives for all plans

- Good communication throughout the organisation

- A performance management culture

- A specific timetable for planning at all levels

- Regular and thorough consultation with all parts of the community

- Analysis and feedback of consultation results

- Regular monitoring and review to ensure the plans are delivering results

The Best Value Performance Plan should be the end result of a planning process that has included understanding what Best Value means within the authority, undertaking service reviews in order to deliver Best Value services, establishing appropriate performance indicators that give a real measure of performance, and developing action plans that really deliver service improvement to achieve targets.

Exercise 6

Assessing Your Best Value Performance Plan

Obtain a copy of the performance plan that was distributed to the public and make an objective assessment by answering the following questions and assigning a score from one to ten, where one is very poor and 10 is excellent.

	Yes/No	Score
Does it contain information with respect to all of the main headings identified at the beginning of this chapter?		
Is there a clear vision?		
Is it easy to read?		
Is it concise?		
Are the objectives SMART (see page 69)?		
Has there been wide ranging consultation?		
Has there been staff involvement?		
Is it accessible to all parts of the community?		
Has it been well communicated?		
Has there been any feedback?		
Are the targets realistic?		

	Yes/No	Score
Is it well presented and highly visual?		
Are management and staff committed to achieving the targets within the plan?		
Is the plan consistent with other plans?		
Is there a process for monitoring the plan?		
Has the plan (or planning process) had an impact on the organisational culture?		

For analysis of scores see suggested solutions (page 83)

As a result of the above assessment, set out your recommendations for improvements to the Best Value Performance Plan and the Planning process

Improvements to the Plan

Improvements to the Planning Process

SOLUTIONS
TO
EXERCISES

Solutions to Exercises

Suggested Solution to Exercise 1
Diagnostic Questionnaire ~ Where are we now - in terms of Best Value?~ 81

Suggested Solution to Exercise 6
Assessing Your Best Value Performance Plan 83

Suggested Solution to Exercise 1

Diagnostic Questionnaire
~ Where are we now - in terms of Best Value?~

How to score:

For each (✔) award 5 points and for each (✗) award 0 points. If the (n/a) column has been used then 2 points should be given. Total the score and consider where you are in terms of Best Value from one of the following paragraphs.

Score 85 – 100

Many of the building blocks for Best Value are already in place and the seeds of a performance culture have already been sown. In order to achieve Best Value for all service areas, there must be a vision of what Best Value means for the authority which is understood by staff and the community. The service review process will provide a useful framework for continuous improvement. If practical action plans are put in place to achieve realistic targets, you should easily be able to move forward towards being in the top quartile performing authorities (if you are not already there).

Score 60 – 84

Some of the attributes required for Best Value are in place, however, there are still a number of areas where basic work needs to be done. It is important that a foundation for Best Value is established as this makes the process of undertaking Best Value reviews, developing performance indicators, setting targets, monitoring and measuring results and implementing action plans more effective. There may be a need to change the culture within the organisation to ensure that it focuses on customer needs and performance. This change will only be achieved over time and must be part of the overall Best Value approach. You are not yet a Best Value service but having identified the areas with a '0' score, this is a good starting point for future improvement and development.

Score below 60

Unfortunately there is a lot of work ahead in order to become a Best Value service and an immediate need to begin addressing certain fundamental areas with respect to objectives, targets, unit costing, customer satisfaction, and so on. The service review process is likely to be more difficult and time consuming due to the lack of information currently available, and hence the results of the review will most probably be more challenging. Organisational change will be a definite result of this process. Realistic timescales need to be set and research into the way other authorities are achieving Best Value will be useful.

Suggested Solution to Exercise 6

Assessing Your Best Value Performance Plan

Score 120 – 160

You obviously have an excellent Best Value performance plan which will need very little modification year on year to keep it up to date and fresh. For areas where the scores are less than 10, there is still room for some improvement. Comments as to how improvements can be made should be fed into the appropriate area. Ideally this assessment should take place on an annual basis for each new plan, and the total score compared year on year. The results of the assessment should get closer and closer to perfection. It should be remembered that the plan is only successful if it is used and implemented. Hopefully a high score has also been given to the process of monitoring the plan to ensure that the plan is working and delivering the desired results.

Score 80 – 119

This score reflects a performance plan that may be adequate but has significant scope for improvement. If the areas of weakness include consultation, communication and feedback, there will be a need for an authority wide strategy to tackle these issues which should result in a change in the organisational culture. If low scores have been obtained on presentation and content issues, there may be a need to review how the plan has been developed. Priority should be given to areas where scores are below 5, as this score is not acceptable and corrective action should definitely have been taken in time for the following year. Best Value is about continuous improvement generally and you should be working towards higher scores in all areas year on year.

Score Less than 80

The Best Value performance plan is clearly not of the required standard and it is likely that the audit and inspection team will have detailed comments to make. If the plan is a reflection of how the Best Value process has been implemented, there may be serious consequences, for example, if there is a lack of proper consultation, or if there are no specific objectives. In certain cases the Secretary of State has powers of intervention that can be invoked where there is clear evidence of any failure in the process. Although a single failure is unlikely to trigger intervention, a failure of substance may cause intervention. Failures of substance include the following:

❖ Failure to meet any single nationally prescribed standard of performance

❖ Persistently high unit costs (in comparison with other organisations) not justified by higher quality services or greater needs

❖ Failure to improve service standards or a deterioration in standards

❖ Failure to draw up and implement an action plan following a critical inspection report

Although on the performance plan a poor score may not be due to any failures in process or substance, it does show the need for significant improvements to be made as soon as possible to ensure that such failures do not re-occur.

INDEX

Index

A

Action Plans 17, 70
Audit 8, 65
Audit and Inspection Process 5
Audit Commission 50, 51

B

Best Value 3
Best Value Principles 40
Business Plan 71

C

Central Government 5
Challenge 14
Commitment 70
Communicating the Plan 67
Communication 41, 71
Community Plan 67, 71
Comparative Information 18
   Example 21
Compare 18
Compete 29
Consult 22
Consultation 45
Consultation Methods 22, 24
Consultation Statement 65
Corporate Plan 71
Cost Efficiency 51
Cost per Unit 18, 41
Current Performance 64
Cycle for Performance Monitoring *60*

D

Data Collection 52, 57
Definition of Best Value
   Aim 5
   Consultation 6

Performance 6
Service Improvement 7
Service Provision 6
Services 5
Use of Resources 7
Delivering Services 1
Department for the Environment Transport and Regio 50, 51, 63, 64
Developing a Vision 68
Developing the Performance Plan 68

E

Economy 1, 14
Effective Consultation 27
Effectiveness 14
Efficiency 1, 14, *51*, 64
External Consultants 13
External Provider 39

F

Fair Access 51
Financial Plan 71
Financial Statement 66
Focus Groups 26, 67
Four 'C's 6, 11
   Challenge 14
   Compare 18
   Compete 29
   Consult 22
Framework 4
Fundamental Service Review 11

G

Government 51

I

In-house Provider 39
Inspection Report 65
Internet 26, 67
Interviews 25

L

Leadership 68
Local Businesses 24
Local Meetings 26

Local People 24, 63, 70
Local Performance Indicators 51
Local Standards 11

M

Measurement 52, *57. See also Performance Measurement*
Measuring Progress 69, 70
Mixed Economy 40
Monitoring 52

N

National Indicators 50
National Standards 11
Newsletters 27

O

Objectives 64, 71
Open Market 40
Operational Plan 71

P

Panels 26
Partnerships 40
Performance 18, 51, 64
Performance Indicators 18, 49, 52, 56
  Audit Commission 50
  Best Value 50
  Local 50, 52
  Local People 51
Performance Management 40, 71
  Framework 4
Performance Measurement *57*, 69
Performance Monitoring 59
  Cycle *60*
Performance Plan 5, 8, 63, 70
  Development 68
  Format 66
  Process. *See also* Planning Process
Performance Standards 16, 49
Performance Targets 11, 50, 56, 70
Planning Process 68
Productivity Levels 19

Q

Quality 51, 52
Quality Improvement 4
Quality Standards 16
Questionnaires 24, 67

R

Review 52, 65

S

Satisfaction Ratings 18
Service Delivery 39, 51
Service Improvement 60
Service Objectives 52
Service Plan 71
Service Providers 23
Service Review 11, 17, 31
   Objectivity 31
Service Reviews 69
Service Strategy 15
Service Users 23
Services 4, 37
Setting Priorities 69
Setting Targets 69
SMART Objectives 69
Specialist Unit 13
Staff 23
Staff Survey 67
Standard Approach 4
Strategic Plan 71
Strategy Objectives 51

T

Target Setting 56, 59
Targets 65, 69
Technology 57

V

Vision 4, 70, 71

NATIONAL
POLICE
LIBRARY